First World War
and Army of Occupation
War Diary
France, Belgium and Germany

60 DIVISION
Headquarters, Branches and Services
Adjutant and Quarter-Master General
28 December 1914 - 23 March 1915

WO95/3026/3

The Naval & Military Press Ltd
www.nmarchive.com
Published in association with The National Archives

Published by

The Naval & Military Press Ltd

Unit 10 Ridgewood Industrial Park,

Uckfield, East Sussex,

TN22 5QE England

Tel: +44 (0) 1825 749494

www.naval-military-press.com

www.nmarchive.com

This diary has been reprinted in facsimile from the original. Any imperfections are inevitably reproduced and the quality may fall short of modern type and cartographic standards.

© Crown Copyright
Images reproduced by permission of The National Archives, London, England, 2015.

Contents

Document type	Place/Title	Date From	Date To
Heading	WO95/3026/3		
Heading	War Diary of the D.A.A & Q.M.G 2/2nd London Division From 28th Dec 14 To 31st Jany 15 Volume 6		
War Diary	Reigate Dorking	28/12/1914	28/12/1914
War Diary	Redhill Horley	31/12/1914	31/12/1914
War Diary	Redhill	31/12/1914	31/12/1914
War Diary	Reigate Betchworth	02/01/1915	02/01/1915
War Diary	Nutfield	02/01/1915	02/01/1915
War Diary	Reigate	02/01/1915	04/01/1915
War Diary	Dorking	04/01/1915	07/01/1915
War Diary	Redhill	08/01/1915	12/01/1915
War Diary	Betchworth Park Reigate Heath Earlswood Common	12/01/1915	12/01/1915
War Diary	Maidstone	13/01/1915	19/01/1915
War Diary	Epsom	22/01/1915	26/01/1915
War Diary	Orford Reigate Redhill	27/01/1915	31/01/1915
War Diary	Reigate	02/02/1915	02/02/1915
War Diary	London	08/02/1915	08/02/1915
War Diary	Wonham	09/02/1915	09/02/1915
War Diary	Dorking	09/02/1915	17/02/1915
War Diary	Sandwich	18/02/1915	18/02/1915
War Diary	London	22/02/1915	22/02/1915
War Diary	Maidstone to London	23/02/1915	23/02/1915
War Diary	Reigate Redhill to Hyth	23/02/1915	23/02/1915
War Diary	Sandwich	24/02/1915	24/02/1915
War Diary	Nutfield	25/02/1915	25/02/1915
War Diary	London to Dorking	23/02/1915	28/02/1915
War Diary	Hyth to Reigate Redhill	23/02/1915	28/02/1915
War Diary	Leatherhead	03/03/1915	03/03/1915
War Diary	St Albans	09/03/1915	09/03/1915
War Diary	Sandwich	10/03/1915	10/03/1915
War Diary	Reigate	11/03/1915	11/03/1915
War Diary	Dorking	12/03/1915	12/03/1915
War Diary	St Albans	13/03/1915	13/03/1915
War Diary	Reigate	15/03/1915	19/03/1915
War Diary	Watford	22/03/1915	22/03/1915
War Diary	Reigate	23/03/1915	23/03/1915
War Diary	Watford	29/03/1915	29/03/1915
War Diary	St Albans	29/03/1915	29/03/1915
War Diary	Hatfield	29/03/1915	29/03/1915
War Diary	Radlett	29/03/1915	29/03/1915
War Diary	Watford	30/03/1915	30/03/1915
War Diary	St Albans	30/03/1915	30/03/1915
War Diary	Hatfield	30/03/1915	30/03/1915
War Diary	St Albans	30/03/1915	31/03/1915
Miscellaneous	Statement for February 1915		
War Diary	2/13th London Rgt	30/01/1915	28/03/1915
War Diary	2/14th London Rgt	26/01/1915	17/03/1915
War Diary	2/16th London Rgt	23/01/1915	23/03/1915

WO 95/3026/3

Confidential

War Diary

of

The D.A.A. & Q.M.G.

2/2 nd London Division

from 28th Dec '14 to 31st Jany '15.

1914 DEC — 1915 FEB   Volume E

Army Form C. 2118.

WAR DIARY
or
INTELLIGENCE SUMMARY.
(Erase heading not required.)

Instructions regarding War Diaries and Intelligence Summaries are contained in F. S. Regs., Part II. and the Staff Manual respectively. Title pages will be prepared in manuscript.

Place	Date	Hour	Summary of Events and Information	Remarks and references to Appendices
REIGATE DORKING	1914 29 Dec		2/2nd London T.S. Column to Billets at REIGATE & DORKING	
REDHILL HORLEY	31st		2/6th London Infy Bgde to Billets at REDHILL and HORLEY.	
REDHILL	1915 2nd Jan		2/6th London F.A. to Billets at REDHILL.	
REIGATE BETCHWORTH	2/1st		2/1st London Infy Bgde to Billets at REIGATE & BETCHWORTH.	
NUTFIELD	3/2		2/2nd London Div. RE to Billets at NUTFIELD.	
REIGATE	2/3rd		2/3rd London F.A. to Billets at REIGATE.	
REIGATE	4th		H.Q. 2/2nd London Division to Billets at REIGATE.	
DORKING			2/4th London Infy Bgde bus 2/13th & 2/16th London Rgt to Billets at DORKING.	
DORKING	5th		2/4th London F.A. to Billets at DORKING.	
REDHILL	7th		1 Capt. 3 Sub. 2/14th London Rgt. ordered to join 1/14th London Rgt.	
	8th		2/17th, 2/18th, 2/19th, 2/21st, 2/22nd Employed on Entrenching work REDHILL position by 2 Batts.	
	12th		Inspection by G.O.C. i/c Central Force & G.O.C. 2nd Army.	
BETCHWORTH PARK HEATH			2/4th London Infy Bde bus (2/13th & 2/16th?) at BETCHWORTH PARK	
REIGATE PARK EARLSWOOD COMMON		9.45 AM	2/5 4th London Infy Bgde at REIGATE HEATH	
			2/6th London Infy Bde at EARLSWOOD COMMON.	
MAIDSTONE	13th		2/13th & 2/16th London Rgt to Billets at MAIDSTONE.	
	14th		Draft of 400 all ranks 2/14th London Rgt. ordered to be held in readiness to proceed to join 1/14th London Rgt.	
	15th		Officers 1 Capt. 3 Sub. 2/14th London Rgt. ordered to proceed with draft to join 1/14th London Rgt.	
			Draft formed by 2/14th London Rgt. cancelled.	See 7th inst.

Army Form C. 2118.

WAR DIARY
or
INTELLIGENCE SUMMARY.
(Erase heading not required.)

Instructions regarding War Diaries and Intelligence Summaries are contained in F. S. Regs., Part II and the Staff Manual respectively. Title pages will be prepared in manuscript.

Place	Date 1915	Hour	Summary of Events and Information	Remarks and references to Appendices
	16th Jany		Nr. Wrigglesworth unposted Lieut. R.A.M.C. T. attached 2/7th London Rgt returning by G.O.C.'s orders.	
	17"		Inspection of Billets by Col. Dickinson Member Central Billeting Comtee	
	18"		Inspection of Billets by Col. Dickinson Member Central Billeting Comtee	
	19"		O.C. 2/16th reports 1 Capt. 2 Sub. 245 other ranks equipped & ready to proceed to join 1/16th London Rgt. Inspection of Billets by Col. Dickinson Member Central Billeting Comtee	
EPSOM	22nd	9.30 a.m.	Inspection of 2/2nd London Div. Engrs 2/13th London Rgt on Epsom Downs by Secty of State for War	
	25"		1 Capt. 2 Sub's 2/16th London Rgt. Ordered to proceed to join 1/16th London Rgt. independently of draft	
	26"		Japanese Rifles & 100 rounds S.A.A. rifle issued to Battalions of this Division	
ORFORD REIGATE REDHILL	27"		2/14th from Worthing 2/16th from Maidstone 2/23rd 2/24th from Horley Employed entraining for all London Docton 2/16th at ORFORD 2/14" & 2/23rd 2/24th at REIGATE REDHILL	
			Additional reinforcement for Expeditionary force ordered. 2/13th 192 in addition to those already ordered. 2/14" 487 2/16" 19.	
	31st		1 Section 2/13th ordered proceed Southampton to report to Commandant for orders to proceed to FRANCE.	

A O Lynch ff Lt Col
D.A. + A.D.M.G. 2/2nd London Div

Army Form C. 2118.

WAR DIARY
or
INTELLIGENCE SUMMARY.
(Erase heading not required.)

Instructions regarding War Diaries and Intelligence Summaries are contained in F.S. Regs., Part II and the Staff Manual respectively. Title pages will be prepared in manuscript.

Place	Date 1915.	Hour	Summary of Events and Information	Remarks and references to Appendices
REIGATE	2nd		Divisional Head Quarters moved to "The Barons" REIGATE.	
LONDON	8th		Allotted Staff Conference at WAR OFFICE re march of XII & XXIII Divisions.	
WONHAM	9th		C.o.c of C.S.M. reported on 2/20th WONHAM	
DORKING	"		C.o.c of C.S.M. reported in 4/4th DORKING	
	15th		Draft 1 Off. 65 other ranks 2/16th proceeded to join Expeditionary Force.	
	17th		Draft 5 Officers 2/4th proceeded to join Expeditionary Force.	
SANDWICH	18th		C.o.c C.S.M. reported in 2/4th SANDWICH	
LONDON	22nd		2/11th, 2/15th, 2/11th F.A. from DORKING to LONDON to clear room for march of XII, XXIII Divisions.	
	23rd		2/13th, 2/16th from MAIDSTONE to LONDON to clear room for march of XII & XXIII Divisions.	
MAIDSTONE to LONDON				
REIGATE REDHILL to HYTH	24th		1000 men of the 2/15th & 2/16th Bgde from REIGATE, REDHILL to HYTH for musketry. to clear room for march of XII – XXIII Divisions. –	
SANDWICH	26th		Draft 2 conducting officers 126 other ranks 2/13 & 6 Join Expeditionary Force. C.o.c C.S.M 2/4th SANDWICH.	
NUTFIELD	25th		C.o.c. C.S.M. 2nd London Div. R.E. NUTFIELD.	
LONDON to DORKING	28th		2/11th, 2/15th, 2/4th & F.A. from LONDON to DORKING	
HYTH to REIGATE REDHILL	28th		1000 men of the 2/15th 2/16th Bgde from HYTH to REIGATE - REDHILL.	

Army Form C. 2118.

March 1915.
WAR DIARY
or
~~INTELLIGENCE SUMMARY~~
(Erase heading not required.)

Instructions regarding War Diaries and Intelligence Summaries are contained in F. S. Regs., Part II. and the Staff Manual respectively. Title pages will be prepared in manuscript.

Place	Date	Hour	Summary of Events and Information	Remarks and references to Appendices
Leatherhead.	3rd		Move of 2/13th London Rgt from billets at Peace Station LONDON to billets at LEATHERHEAD.	
St Albans	9th		Parties from all units of the Division sent to St Albans Billeting Area to take over Stores, Horses, Vehicles, etc from 1st Line units serving with 1/2nd London Division.	
Sandwich	10th		6 Officers 240 other ranks from 2/4th Lond. Inf. Bde DORKING for Musketry New Rifle Course	
Reigate	11th		Orders received for Division to be prepared to move to St Albans Billeting Area.	
Dorking	12th		6 officers 240 other rank from 2/4th L. Inf. Bde from SANDWICH having completed Musketry Course. No further parties to be sent.	
St Albans	13th		Advanced Billeting Parties from all units to St ALBANS Billeting Area.	
Reigate.	15th		Captain Napier R of O. reported as GSO 3rd grade. Lt Colonel A Dunlop RA reported as GSO 1st grade.	
Reigate	16th		Major P. O'Connor RE reported as GSO 2nd grade	
Reigate.	19th		Major C Spearman struck off strength of Division from GSO 2nd grade	
Watford.	22nd		Move by march route of 2/16th London Rgt from billets at Peace Station London to WATFORD.	
Reigate	23rd		Digging on the South LONDON Defence Position suspended.	
Watford.	29th		Move of HQ 2/4th Lond Inf Bde 2/14th 2/15th from DORKING to WATFORD.	
St Albans.	29th		Move of Div HQ. HQ 2/5th Lond Inf Bde 2/17th 2/18th 2/19th London Rgt from REDHILL to St ALBANS	
St Albans	29th		Move of 2/21st London Rgt from REIGATE to St ALBANS	
Hatfield	29th		Move of 2/23rd London Rgt from HORLEY to HATFIELD.	
RADLETT	29th		Move of 2/4th London F Coy RE from NUTFIELD to RADLETT	

March 1915

WAR DIARY
INTELLIGENCE SUMMARY

Army Form C. 2118.

Place	Date	Hour	Summary of Events and Information	Remarks and references to Appendices
WATFORD.	30th		Move of 2/13th London Regt from LEATHERHEAD to WATFORD.	
WATFORD	30th		Move of 2/4th London F.Amb. from DORKING to WATFORD.	
St ALBANS	30th		Move of 2/19th London Regt from REIGATE to St ALBANS.	
St ALBANS	30th		Move of 2/20th London Regt from BETCHWORTH to St ALBANS	
St ALBANS	30th		Move of 2/22nd London Regt & 2/6th London FAmb & HQ 2/6th London Inf Bde from REDHILL to St ALBANS	
HATFIELD	30th		Move of 2/24th London Regt from HORLEY to HATFIELD.	
St ALBANS	30th		Move of 2/2nd London Signal Coy from NUTFIELD to St ALBANS	
St ALBANS	31st		Move of 2/2nd London T&S column & 2/5th London F.Amb. from REIGATE to St ALBANS.	

Statement for February
1915.

Unit   DAA & QMG. G
Brigade   —
Division   2/2nd London Division
Mobilization Centre. — —
Temporary War Stations   Horley — Redhill — Reigate — Dorking — Maidstone

Discipline   Satisfactory.

Lack of room   C.O's report great difficulty in obtaining
in Detention   admissions to Detention Barracks for men
Barracks   who have received sentences of Detention
                ~~Prisoners have to be kept in rooms of~~
                ~~unsuitable hours~~
                When troops are billeted provision should
                be made for the reception of prisoners
                undergoing short sentences of detention & also
                awaiting trial by Court Martial.
                A room in a house in which the Battalion
                Quarter Guard is accommodated is not
                satisfactory. 3 cases of men so confined have
                ~~having~~ occurred & the men have been tried
                by Court Martial for the offence.
                I think that the provision of Army Act

Forfeiture of   46.(2)(d) forfeiture of all ordinary pay up
Pay. AA 46(2)(d) to 28 days might be more impressed on C.O's

Field Punishment Field Punishment No 2 which C.O's are
                authorized to give is difficult to carry out
                & has been found by experience ~~to be~~ that
                the prisoner only loses some days instruction.

Court Martial   In New Formations Officers have insufficient
Duties   knowledge of Court Martial Duties. In this
                Division this is particularly marked. The
                Form of Court Martial as set out in the
                Manual of Military Law is so complicated as
                to be practically useless. Some few simpler
                form might with advantage be compiled &
                included in future editions.
                It would be well to appoint some selected

Staff Officer as Permanent Deputy Judge Advocate General. He would then be able to be present at all Court Martials to keep the proceedings in order.

Provision of Army Act sec 183 para 2 might ~~with~~ be made more use of especially in ~~unit police with NCOs~~ embodied Territorial Units. Many Territorial N.C.O. were just capable of performing their duties during peace time, but when once embodied were been found to be incapable. Reduction under this Section of the Army Act avoids the stain which is connected by Court Martial in bound to leave

Very stringent disciplinary powers have been conferred in the Case of Officers, somewhat similar powers already existed in the case of N.C.Os but are not made use of.

Deputy Judge Advocate General

Reduction of N.C.O by G.O.C. in C. AA 183·(2)

† **Administration**

① <u>Medical Services</u>

The Territorial Army is bound to ~~suffer~~ from a want of Medical Officers seeing that the pay offered is not so high as that offered for Medical Officers in the new Army.

On appointment a ~~Lieutenant~~ R.A.M.C T receives 14/- a day pay whereas a Lieutenant of the R.A.M.C. New Army receives 24/-

4 the outfit allowance in the R.A.M.C T is £50 but in the new Army £100.

② <u>Channels of Correspondence in routine matters.</u>

Any correspondence from a Battalion which is likely to be forwarded to the War Office, has to be set out in 6 copies as each office through which the correspondence passes retains a copy, & one copy has to be kept in the office of issue

This is particularly cumbersome as Carbon paper will not ~~easily~~ multiplicate more the 5 copies

Would it not be possible to establish a central registry in every Army as is now

Acre in Commands.
Much of the correspondence is of no real interest & is put away & not wanted again.

To give an example of the mass of correspondence that has been dealt with in the last two month: the Divisional Office number on the 4th January was 515 it is now on the 3rd March. A 1202. Q 88 G 90 or a total of 867 in two months.

This mass of correspondence has been dealt with by 3 officers 1 sergt major & 3 clerks.

Army Form C. 2118.

Reinforcement
January to March 1915.
WAR DIARY
or
INTELLIGENCE SUMMARY
(Erase heading not required.)

Instructions regarding War Diaries and Intelligence Summaries are contained in F.S. Regs., Part II. and the Staff Manual respectively. Title pages will be prepared in manuscript.

Rgt.	Date	Hour	Summary of Events and Information		Remarks and references to Appendices
			officers	other ranks.	
2/13ᵗʰ London Rgt.	30ᵗʰ Jan.		To 1/13ᵗʰ London Rgt.	—	206	
do	7ᵗʰ Feb.		do	2	125.	
do.	24ᵗʰ Feb		do	2.	15	
do.	9ᵗʰ Mar		do	—	—	
do.	19ᵗʰ Mar.		do.	4	47.	
do.	29ᵗʰ Mar.		do.	1		10 officers 393 other ranks.
2/14ᵗʰ London Rgt.	26ᵗʰ Jan.		To 1/14ᵗʰ London Rgt.	5	—	
do	17ᵗʰ Feb		do	5	—	
do	7ᵗʰ Mar.		do	1	130.	
do.	17ᵗʰ Mar.		do	3	253	14 officers 383 other ranks.
2/16ᵗʰ London Rgt.	23ʳᵈ Jan		To 1/16ᵗʰ London Rgt.	3	245	
do	15ᵗʰ Feb.		do	1	65.	
do	16ᵗʰ Mar.		do	2	—	
do	23ʳᵈ Mar.		do	1	—	7 officers 310 other ranks.

1577 Wt. W10794/1773 50,000 1/15 D.D. & L. A.D.S.S./Forms/C. 2118.